NATIONAL GEOGRAPHIC KIDS

weird but true!

Stupid Criminals

150 brainless baddies BUSTED, plus wacky facts

Illustrations by Tom Nick Cocotos

NATIONAL
GEOGRAPHIC

WASHINGTON, D.C.

Table of Contents

Window Pain

WINDSOR, ONTARIO, IN CANADA

IT'S UNLAWFUL TO WAKE UP A BEAR TO TAKE ITS PICTURE IN ALASKA.

A robber tried to squeeze through a store window that was so tiny that he got stuck—*really* stuck. After trying to free himself for hours, the would-be thief yelled for help. Arriving later, the owner heard his cries and called police. Officers raced to the scene to pull the robber out. "He was covered in scrapes and cuts," says Staff Sergeant Ed McNorton. "I've never seen a criminal so happy to see the police!"

Bloodhounds—which can be trained to sniff out clues at crime scenes—have 230 million

scent receptors in their noses. That is **40 times the number in the human nose!**

What's the largest art theft in U.S. history? Thirteen paintings worth an estimated $300

ALL WET
LEVITTOWN, NEW YORK

One business owner thought he was about to be robbed—until the thief's "gun" started dripping water. He was being robbed with a water pistol! "The owner realized he was in no danger, except of getting wet," Detective Raymond Cote says. After the businessman refused to hand over any cash, the thief ran away. But police later tracked the guy down. Looks like the thief went from being top gun to little squirt!

A **POLICE DOG** IS CALLED A **K-9**, SHORT FOR **CANINE.**

million, stolen in 1990 from the Isabella Stewart Gardner Museum in Massachusetts.

"Paws-itive" ID

ELK GROVE VILLAGE, ILLINOIS

TWO THIEVES STOLE ABOUT 350,000 SNAILS FROM A WHOLESALER IN POLAND.

Some people will do anything to avoid walking the dog! One teenager was taking his pooch for a stroll when he noticed a neighbor drive away. Seeing the house was empty, the hopeful thief forced his way inside. "But the owner came home a few minutes later," says Sergeant Michael Kirkpatrick. The sneak escaped through the nearest exit but forgot one important thing: his dog! Using the dog's identification tags, police tracked down the intruder. Talk about being in the doghouse!

Al Capone—legendary gangster and mob boss in Chicago, Illinois—was nicknamed

Scarface because he had three scars on his face as a result of injuries from a fight.

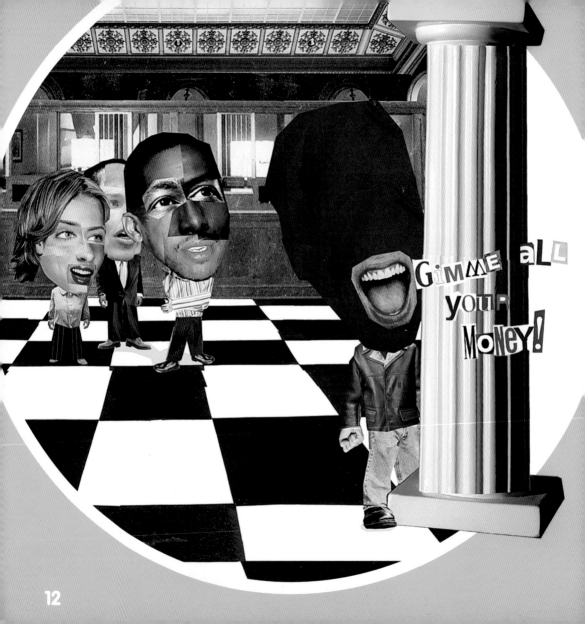

GimmE aLL youR MoNEy!

The Blind Bandit

MODESTO, CALIFORNIA

This unsuccessful bank robber thought he was pretty smart when he decided to disguise his face with fabric. But he forgot one very important thing. To cut eyeholes! In order to see what he was doing, the bad guy had to lift up the fabric, showing everyone in the bank his face. Based on an eyewitness description, it wasn't hard for the cops to track down the "masked" man.

A GROUP OF **ROBBERS IN TAMPA, FLORIDA, WORE SINKS ON THEIR HEADS** AS DISGUISES.

Seagulls are called the "pirates of the seashore" because they often steal food from beachgoers.

What's for DINNER?

ANDERSON, SOUTH CAROLINA

Most criminals will break into an empty house, steal some stuff, and get out fast. But this burglar fried up some mini hot dogs and mixed a jug of juice! When a neighbor checking on the house found the wieners sizzling on the stove, she knew something was up. Police arrived and found the intruder hiding upstairs. They arrested him and made him feel right at home—in jail!

IT'S ILLEGAL TO **BOWL** ON THE SIDEWALK IN **CHICO, CALIFORNIA.**

Fred the baboon steals food from unlocked cars in Cape Town, South Africa, parking lots.

A Missouri man stole a two-karat diamond ring worth $20,000! He swallowed the loot

Dumpster DIVING

DILLON, SOUTH CAROLINA

This crook got caught between a Dumpster and a hard place. He had broken into a junkyard to steal copper wiring and crawled underneath a Dumpster to get it. But once he squeezed in far enough, he couldn't wriggle out! The robber spent the whole night underneath the trash container, and police had to use air bags to lift it high enough to get him out. It's not often that criminals are grateful to the police who arrest them—but this one probably was.

THE **EARLIEST WRITTEN LAWS** DATE BACK TO ROMAN TIMES, **ABOUT 450** B.C.

while police questioned him, but later had to literally cough up the evidence for police.

Roadside Robber

NADDERWATER, ENGLAND, IN THE UNITED KINGDOM

A BANDIT WORE A DARTH VADER MASK TO ROB A BANK IN LONG ISLAND, NEW YORK.

You'd have to be *really* stupid to ask for a ride from the guy you just robbed! When a man found his front door smashed open, he went looking for the culprit. Sure enough, the man spotted the burglar—pushing a wheelbarrow with his stolen stuff in it! Pulling up beside the thief in his car, the man started to confront him. But before he could, the bad guy asked for a ride. The man called police. They were happy to give this thief a lift—right to jail!

A Seattle, Washington robber found himself in a sticky situation when he put his hand in

superglue during a robbery. He escaped, but his fingerprint in the glue made him easy to catch!

A Florida burglar stole a big-screen television and tried to make his getaway on a

Thousand-Dollar Mistake

KALAMAZOO COUNTY, MICHIGAN

Three thieves thought they were pretty smart when they stole a safe full of cash that included a $1,000 bill. After they spent all their small bills, they took the large bill to a bank to break it. But they didn't know that $1,000 bills hadn't been printed since 1945. Figuring the antique money was stolen, the teller contacted police. "The rare bill was a huge red flag," says Detective Sergeant Jim van Dyken. The thieves probably wished a thousand times over that they hadn't been so dumb.

A WOMAN WORE A **CLOWN COSTUME** WHILE TRYING TO **ROB A BANK** IN PENNSYLVANIA.

bicycle. Police arrested the man after becoming suspicious of the oversized cargo.

HIDE-and-SEEK
FERGUS FALLS, MINNESOTA

PIRATES CAN ALSO BE CALLED CORSAIRS, BUCCANEERS, OR FREEBOOTERS.

What's the most logical hiding place if you're robbing a restaurant? One thief thought it would be the oven! After the robber broke into the eatery, the alarms went off and police surrounded the building. Desperate, the thief squeezed into the oven while police searched the place. Officers eventually found him and arrested him on the spot. This bungling bad guy was really bent out of shape!

Thieves stole a meerkat from the Kansas City Zoo by bundling it in a stroller like a

They later left the animal at a local pet store. The staff returned it safely to the zoo.

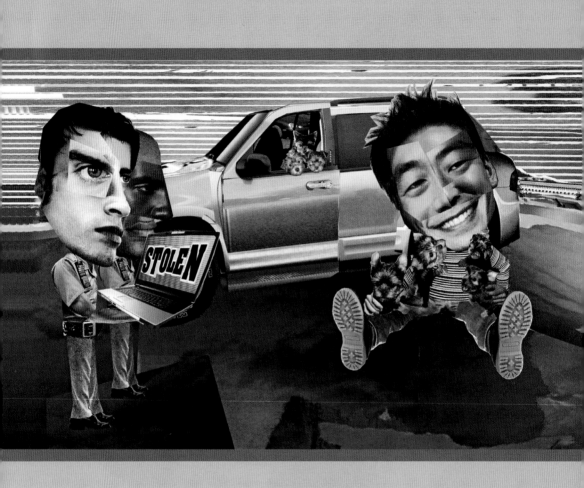

One morning an angry woman broke the drive-through window at a fast-food

In the DOGHOUSE
SAN RAFAEL, CALIFORNIA

Some people never learn. A man who was out on bail for stealing a car drove to the courthouse—in another stolen car! How he got caught was even more stupid: The man left seven dogs in the SUV with the back door open, and some jumped out and started running around the parking lot. Someone called the sheriff's department, who called in the license plate on the crook's car. That's when they discovered it was stolen. Worried about his dogs, the bad guy ran out and asked the police if everything was OK. The dogs? Yes. The guy? No. He's in jail.

A FLORIDA MAN **BROKE IN TO** A HOME AND **BAKED BROWNIES** WHILE THE OWNERS WERE AWAY.

restaurant in Ohio because chicken nuggets weren't served until after 10:30 a.m.

Calling All CROOKS

CHICAGO, ILLINOIS

A **BLACK BEAR** WAS **RESPONSIBLE FOR 21 BREAK-INS** IN MONTANA IN ONE SUMMER.

You shouldn't hand out your phone number to just anybody—especially someone you're trying to rob. While holding up an auto supply shop, a crook discovered that the employees didn't have any cash. He figured the boss would have more money on him. But the boss hadn't come in yet, and the bad guy didn't want to wait. So he gave the employees his phone number. "You better call me when the boss comes," he said before he left. The employees fooled him and called police before they called the crook. When he showed up, the boss was waiting with the cops.

The expression "sent up the river," a slang term for being sent to jail, began in the late 1800s

when criminals were sent up the Hudson River to Sing Sing Prison in Ossining, New York.

Two masked criminals held up a pizzeria in Staten Island, New York. The owners handed

Locked OUT

STANTON, TEXAS

This guy may have thought he was being smart when he locked his getaway car before robbing a drugstore. There was just one problem: The keys were inside, and the car was running. Sprinting out of the store, the robber found he couldn't open his car door and dashed away on foot. Police finally caught him, but he still had his vehicle on his mind. "Would you take care of my car?" he asked police. "It's running, and the keys are in it." Guess they were more interested in locking him up than unlocking his car.

IT'S ILLEGAL TO
WALK A PIG ALONG
MIAMI BEACH IN FLORIDA.

over a bag full of "dough," but the crooks didn't realize it was pizza dough, not money.

STUCK at the Scene

NENDAZ, SWITZERLAND

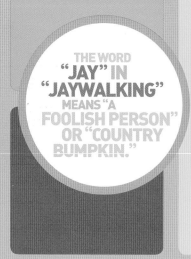

THE WORD "JAY" IN "JAYWALKING" MEANS "A FOOLISH PERSON" OR "COUNTRY BUMPKIN."

Talk about sticking your neck out! When one man finished his late-night stealing spree at a shopping center, he figured he had avoided capture. But the store's automatic doors captured *him*. As the thief tried to leave, the front doors suddenly closed on his neck and foot, trapping him. The crook begged passersby to help pull him out, but they knew what he was up to. So they pushed him inside. Police, however, were more than happy to rescue the thief and throw him in jail.

The largest object ever stolen by an individual was the 10,639-ton cargo ship, the S.S. *Orient*

Trader. The thief slashed the ship's lines and let it drift from the dock to a waiting tugboat.

Photo FINISH

When a crook pretended to help a young woman with directions, he helped himself to her cell phone. Luckily, through special memory technology, police could track everything the thief did with the phone. So when the bad guy snapped a picture of himself with the phone's camera, police accessed the image, publicized the photo, and nabbed him after one of the crook's co-workers turned him in. "As soon as thieves steal cell phones, they use them," says Detective Marcus McNeil. "That makes it easy for us."

A MIAMI WOMAN STOLE $1,600 AND HID THE MONEY IN HER WIG.

Two burglars in Iowa disguised themselves by drawing on their faces with black markers.

LOST and FOUND

EULESS, TEXAS

One thief figured he had everything covered after he robbed a store. But he forgot one thing: his wallet! Detective Marco Valladares found the thief's name and address inside. Then the detective asked the thief to claim his wallet at the lost and found at police headquarters. Amazingly, the thief showed up! Valladares arrested him, but that wasn't the funniest part. Says Valladares, "We don't even *have* a lost and found."

THE U.S. IS HOME TO **A QUARTER** OF THE WORLD'S **PRISON** POPULATION.

Two Minnesota teens were arrested after allegedly stealing 17 calves from barns.

Four men in Wales, United Kingdom, stole $11,000 worth of jewelry from a store. They got

FIND Me!

LAUREL, NEBRASKA

What should your license plate *not* say when you're planning to rob a bank? FINDME! This would-be robber ran away without a cent. But witnesses had no problem describing his getaway truck—and its personalized plate—to police. That was all the police officers needed to find the bad guy. After all, the license plate was begging to be found.

THE WORLD'S MOST STOLEN PAINTING IS A **POCKET-SIZE PORTRAIT BY REMBRANDT** THAT WAS STOLEN FOUR TIMES.

caught when they tried to sell some of the bling back to another branch of the same store.

Hiding in Plain Sight

CHALMETTE, LOUISIANA

IN SOUTH CAROLINA IT'S ILLEGAL FOR KIDS TO PLAY PINBALL.

Hint to thieves: Don't use stolen property to hide stolen property. A family returned home one day to find that their apartment had been robbed. Even their dog's distinctive blue blanket was missing. So of course, when the family spotted the blanket hanging in their neighbors' window, they had a good idea who had stolen their stuff. Police searched the apartment and found clothing and electronics that belonged to the victims. "The crooks were using the blanket as a curtain to hide the stolen property," says Sergeant Jeff Vega. "It was pretty ridiculous."

Surveillance cameras at a Washington State restaurant recorded a man hiding in the

bathroom ceiling until closing time and then nabbing $5,000 from the safe.

A robber's coat was so stuffed with stolen loot that he got stuck trying to escape through a

Dumb, Dumber, and Dumbest

BOSSIER CITY, LOUISIANA

Crime doesn't pay—especially when a thief leaves her purse at the scene. After eating at a Mexican restaurant, four young women took off without paying for their food—and without the purse that belonged to one of them. When officers arrived at the restaurant, they got the name and photo of one of the thieves from the driver's license in the purse. That made it easy to recognize her when she and her pals returned to fetch the forgotten handbag. Guess they were too dumb to notice the police, who were still at the restaurant.

THE TERM "PENITENTIARY" COMES FROM THE WORD "PENANCE."

...e in a fence. When he asked for help, the homeowner he had robbed called police ins...

Santa CROOK

KINGS BEACH, CALIFORNIA

A SEATTLE, WASHINGTON, DOG ATE $1,200 THAT IT FOUND ON TOP OF A DRESSER.

When this thief couldn't break into a house through the doors or windows, he had an idea: lower himself down the chimney. But it *wasn't* his idea to get stuck! After neighbors heard him screaming for help, firefighters used axes to dismantle the chimney brick by brick. The cramped and sooty criminal was happy to be pulled free but *unhappy* to be arrested by police.

A Missouri man tried to rob a bank where his wife was a teller. Her response? "Go home!"

SORRY, Wrong Number

LINCOLNTON, NORTH CAROLINA

When Rick Lynn got a phone call from a criminal asking for something illegal, he wondered what was up. After all, Lynn is a police detective! It turns out the bad guy dialed the detective by mistake, but Lynn didn't let on who he really was. Instead, the smart detective went to the criminal's house—but even then the guy didn't figure out that he was about to be arrested. "I wasn't dealing with a rocket scientist," Lynn says.

A ROBBER GOT **BUSTED** BECAUSE HE **POSTED PICTURES** OF HIS LOOT ON **FACEBOOK.**

A burglar who broke into a safe in Alaska swiped $20,000 but left $80,000 for the owner.

Down the TOILET

STUART, FLORIDA

AUSTRALIA WAS ORIGINALLY A BRITISH PENAL COLONY.

Talk about flush with embarrassment! Officers got a tip that a guy had stolen cash, jewelry, and a weapon. After the man let the officers into his hotel room, Detective Carlo Sciandra asked the nervous suspect if he could use the bathroom. When Sciandra tried to flush the toilet, it didn't work. He lifted the tank's lid to fix the problem—and found the stolen weapon, soaking wet. Sciandra solved the case but also got some unwanted attention. "Now when I walk into the bathroom at work," he says, "I hear lots of jokes."

A bank robber in Dayton, Ohio, tried to make a quick getaway by boarding a city bus.

It didn't take long for police to catch up with him at a bus stop only a half-mile down the road.

Three criminals used spoons to chip through their cell walls in Alcatraz Prison,

Card SHARKS
DES MOINES, IOWA

This is one card trick that didn't fool anyone. After a shopping spree, three "customers" tried to pay for their items with a credit card. But when the cashier looked at the card, she noticed it actually belonged to her! Her credit card had been stolen a few days earlier, so the young woman secretly alerted her boss, who contacted police. That's one cashier who really took *charge* of the situation!

IT'S AGAINST THE LAW TO **BRING A SKUNK** INTO THE STATE OF **TENNESSEE.**

located on an island in San Francisco Bay, California. They were never seen again.

Not-So-Stolen CAR

BALTIMORE, MARYLAND

Most people call police when their car is missing. This guy called police when the car he had *stolen* was missing! When the real owner spotted her stolen car, she had it towed. But when the thief saw that the car he had stolen was gone, he called police! The bad guy had left his wallet, which could tie him to the crime, in the car. So he tried to convince the cops that the car was his. But they knew better. The police arrested the man—*and* kept his wallet!

THERE HAVE BEEN MORE THAN **200 FILMS** ABOUT FICTIONAL DETECTIVE **SHERLOCK HOLMES.**

Sam the seagull became a YouTube sensation when videos showed it repeatedly

snatching bags of chips from a shop in Scotland, U.K. Some locals even paid for its snacks.

Parking Space PICASSO
ALBUQUERQUE, NEW MEXICO

The last place bad guys want to go is jail, right? Well, this one drove a stolen truck to jail to pick up a friend! A passerby noticed that the truck looked a lot like his buddy's and alerted a nearby police officer, who traced the license plate on the spot. Sure enough, it was the stolen vehicle. Police quickly nabbed the risk-taking robber, who had tried to paint the truck before driving it to the jail. The sloppy paint job couldn't hide the crime—or save him from serving the time.

IT'S ILLEGAL TO **SELL A HAUNTED HOUSE** IN **NEW YORK WITHOUT TELLING THE BUYER.**

A Kentucky robber disguised his face with duct tape, but he sweat so much that it fell off.

Down-and-Out

GLOUCESTER, ENGLAND, IN THE UNITED KINGDOM

This criminal probably wished he hadn't run away from the scene of the crime. After he snatched a woman's purse, he ran smack into a brick wall and knocked himself unconscious! When he woke up, he was in the hospital—with two police officers staring at him. They were nice enough to wait for his injuries to heal before arresting him. But you can be sure this bad guy still had a major headache on his hands!

IT'S ILLEGAL TO **HONK YOUR HORN** IN FRONT OF A SANDWICH SHOP AT NIGHT IN **LITTLE ROCK, ARKANSAS.**

"Hot house," a slang term for a jail, may have started at Leavenworth Penitentiary in Kansas

because a bad ventilation system made the building remarkably hot year-round.

A Texas teen ordered a taco at a fast-food drive-through window while robbing the

Litter of the LAW
PASADENA, MARYLAND

Littering is bad for the environment—but sometimes it's good for police. Four thieves who broke into a gas station to steal candy bars and potato chips couldn't wait to sample the snacks. As they munched and crunched, they tossed aside their empty candy wrappers, leaving a trail of trash. An officer, working with a police dog to track the suspects' scents, followed the litter straight to the crooks. What a sweet arrest!

ONLY **EIGHT WOMEN** HAVE EVER BEEN ON **THE FBI'S MOST WANTED LIST.**

cashier. Then he waited for his order to be ready—just enough time for police to arrive!

License to Steal

WEST PALM BEACH, FLORIDA

People forget stuff all the time. But a robber forgetting his wallet at a crime scene? That's exactly what one bad guy did after holding up a convenience store. Distracting the cashier with small talk, the thief absentmindedly placed his wallet on the counter. Suddenly, he demanded money and then bolted from the store—without his wallet. Inside the wallet was his photo ID, which included his name and address. So it didn't take long for the cops to nab the crook.

SHARING A **DRINKING CUP** IN PUBLIC **IS PROHIBITED** IN SEATTLE, WASHINGTON.

term "cat burglar" comes from the catlike moves of crooks who slink around buildi

Customs officials nabbed a counterfeiter who tried to pass off 250 fake one-billion-dollar

Off the CUFF
HASTINGS, NEW ZEALAND

Two heads aren't always better than one. A couple of criminals, handcuffed together as they were led from the courthouse, managed to break free from their guard. There wasn't much time to plan their escape. So when a light pole got in their way, one guy ran to the right, and the other ran to the left. Instead of making a getaway, the cuffed crooks wrapped themselves around the pole, smacked their heads together, and collapsed. Looks like they didn't know what hit them.

A BURGLAR IN DELAWARE **CALLED 911** WHEN HE GOT **LOCKED INSIDE** A HOUSE HE WAS **ROBBING.**

bills as real. What gave him away? There's no such thing as a billion-dollar bill.

TIGHT
Squeeze
DENTON, TEXAS

A GERMAN POLITICIAN STOLE MORE THAN 200 TOILET PAPER ROLLS FROM CITY HALL.

There was no light at the end of *this* tunnel. When police arrived at a house where a trespasser had been reported, the suspect jumped out a window and ran away. During a ten-minute chase, the guy tried to escape by crawling into a drainage pipe. Problem: The pipe was just 24 inches around. Bigger problem: The guy got stuck! He was wedged so tightly that police had to pump air into the pipe so he wouldn't suffocate. Ten hours later, the water department dug him out. The guy was probably relieved to end up in a nice, roomy jail cell.

The *Mona Lisa* painting was stolen from the Louvre Museum in Paris, France, in 1911.

Police searched everyone leaving the country, but the artwork turned up years later in Italy.

Famous gangster John Dillinger stole more than $300,000 from banks all over the

Wanted!
FRUITPORT TOWNSHIP, MICHIGAN

If you're on a scavenger hunt and need a photo of two police officers eating doughnuts, there's no harm in asking, right? Not unless you're a wanted criminal! The bad guy wandered over to his local police station, where two officers agreed to pose for the camera. One of the officers thought the criminal's name sounded familiar. Sure enough, he had seen the guy's picture on a wanted poster, so the officers made a speedy arrest. No more fun and games for this guy!

A TEEN DRESSED AS A COW STOLE 26 GALLONS OF MILK FROM A STORE IN VIRGINIA.

midwestern United States in the 1930s—that's equal to about $4 million in today's money!

NO BAG, No Bucks

NEW HUDSON, MICHIGAN

A SWEDISH MAN NAMED **BOB ARNO** IS KNOWN AS THE WORLD'S FASTEST PICKPOCKET.

Disguise—check. Gloves—check. Money bag—*oops!* One would-be bank robber wasn't as prepared as he thought when he handed a bank teller a note saying, "You know what to do." The teller asked the thief if he had a bag for the money. He didn't. Trying to cooperate, she turned to find something to stash the cash in. But the thief—too embarrassed by his blunder—decided not to hang around and ran out the door empty-handed.

Captain William Kidd—the only real pirate known to have actually buried treasure—hid his loot

on Gardiners Island, New York, in the late 1600s. People are still hunting for the treasure.

In ancient Rome, some criminals were forced to become gladiators as punishment for their

TRAIL to Jail

CEDAR BLUFF, ALABAMA

A group of bank robbers discovered one big flaw in their perfect crime: They left the window of their getaway car open as they were escaping. Stolen cash flew out the car's back window as the foursome blasted down the highway and caught the attention of sheriff's deputies. After the thieves crashed the car, police cornered them and recovered most of the cash. Bet these jailbirds wish they could fly away from prison as fast as their stolen loot flew out the window!

IN **SUN PRAIRIE, WISCONSIN,** IT'S ILLEGAL TO **BIKE** WITH YOUR **HANDS OFF** THE HANDLEBARS.

crimes. They fought and often died in combat in amphitheaters packed with spectators.

Say CHEESE

NORTH RICHLAND HILLS, TEXAS

"Smile, you're on camera!" The sign clearly tells spy shop customers that they're being filmed. But these two thieves must have wanted to be stars. Thirteen video cameras filmed the brothers as they broke into the store, grabbed $8,700 worth of equipment, and drove away in a stolen car. After local TV channels broadcast the video footage, someone identified one of the thieves. These guys might have done better to avoid the spotlight.

THE **LARGEST** AMOUNT OF MONEY **EVER STOLEN FROM A BANK WAS** **$69.8 MILLION.**

A burglar in China tried to scale a five-story apartment building, but he got stuck dangling

from the side. Emergency workers rescued him and delivered him straight to police.

Infamous outlaw Billy the Kid was arrested for the first time as a teenager in 1875.

Sticky FINGERS

LYNCHBURG, VIRGINIA

Table manners are important, even for criminals. One crook took time out for a snack from the refrigerator in a house he was robbing. He left behind the piece of fried chicken he'd been munching, as well as an orange juice bottle with his greasy fingerprints all over it. Once police had the prints, it was a cinch to figure out the identity of the burglar and arrest him. "He certainly made things easier," says Captain Brandon Zuidema. Bet this guy wishes he'd cleaned up his mess after he was done eating!

THERE WERE **445** PIRATE ATTACKS IN 2010, THE MOST ON RECORD IN ONE YEAR.

His crime? Legend has it he stole a basket of laundry in Silver City, New Mexico.

Crime-Fighting HERD

SCHÖNBERG, GERMANY

IN SINGAPORE YOU CAN GET SENTENCED TO **THREE MONTHS IN JAIL** FOR JAYWALKING.

This car thief discovered that police officers aren't the only ones who can corner a criminal. After stealing a car, two bad guys led police on a car chase to the edge of a forest, where the thieves took off on foot. The passenger was caught right away, but the driver kept running and ran smack into a herd of toothy wild boars. Surrounded by the angry animals—which were probably trying to protect their babies—the criminal yelled for help. Officers shouted and shooed the boars off. And then they hauled the thief to jail.

An April Fools' Day prankster "captured" an unsuspecting victim when he put glue on a toilet

seat in a Maryland shopping center. Now will the second-degree assault charges also stick?

How to crack this safe

HP 1740

A millionaire in Switzerland got a speeding ticket for $290,000 after driving a Ferrari

CAUGHT in the Web

WILMINGTON, DELAWARE

This guy learned his lesson: Always do your homework. A man who tried to break into a restaurant safe strolled into the building, hid in the ceiling, and waited for the restaurant to close. He thought cracking the safe would be easy money—until he realized he didn't know how. So he logged onto the office computer and searched for instructions online. By the time he found them—and a drill to crack the safe—he was way behind schedule. Two managers walked in and caught him in the act. Now he probably googles "jail-time activities."

THE OLDEST CONVICTED BANK ROBBER WAS 92 YEARS OLD.

85 miles an hour through a village! Fines in Switzerland are based on a person's wealth

Fashion Felon
ELK GROVE, CALIFORNIA

One inmate liked his jail uniform so much that he took it with him after he was released—and got himself thrown back in jail because of it! The former prisoner decided to wear his favorite outfit in town, but alarmed residents thought he was an escaped inmate and called police. When he admitted that he had smuggled the uniform out of jail by wearing it under his regular clothes, police sent him right back to jail—for stealing county property.

IN CHEYENNE, WYOMING, IT'S ILLEGAL TO OWN MORE THAN FOUR DOGS.

When a homeowner in Sacramento, California, walked in on a burglar, the thief scrambled

for a cover story. She told the startled homeowner that she actually lived in the house.

"Smishing" is the term for a scam in which a criminal texts or calls mobile phones in

Rap ATTACK
DUBLIN, GEORGIA

One criminal said he never attacked anyone—but he *sang* a different story. He wrote a rap song claiming credit for the crime, and even named his victim in the tune! "He bragged about what he did in his song," says Brandon Faircloth, deputy chief assistant district attorney. "That definitely did not work in the criminal's favor." Now the bad guy is singing the blues—the jailhouse blues.

THE TERM "MUG SHOT" COMES FROM THE 18TH-CENTURY BRITISH SLANG TERM *MUG*, MEANING "FACE."

order to gather the owners' personal information and access their bank accounts.

SNAGGED
WICHITA, KANSAS

This guy wasn't only arrested—he was nailed! When police arrived on the scene of a suspected robbery, they realized the burglar was still inside the building. So they waited by a back door with a suspicious hole in it. Suddenly, stolen items came flying out of the hole, and the burglar soon followed. But as he tried to crawl out of the hole, his pants snagged on a nail and he had to leave them behind. The police waiting for the crook nabbed him, minus his pants.

OCTOPUSES IN AQUARIUMS SOMETIMES SNEAK INTO THEIR NEIGHBORS' TANKS TO STEAL SNACKS.

A carrier pigeon was trained to fly illegal packages into a prison in Colombia. Prison officials

uncovered the plot when a package was so heavy that the bird could not fly.

SPELLING Counts

HILLSBORO, OREGON

Good thing this bandit didn't pay attention when learning her letters. The crook entered a bank and handed the teller a scribbled note demanding cash. Trouble was, the handwriting was so messy and had so many misspelled words that the teller said she couldn't read the note. The hopeful thief didn't give up and started to write another one. While she was busy rewriting, the teller pressed the silent alarm button. Police arrived just in time. Maybe she can work on her penmanship in prison.

THE NFL FINED A PLAYER **$25,000** FOR POSTING TWITTER UPDATES DURING A GAME.

Looters at an Egyptian museum stole gift shop replicas, thinking they were the real artifacts.

Take-Out ORDER

CINCINNATI, OHIO

One thief discovered he should've left his wallet at home while he robbed a fast-food joint. He'd pulled out his wallet as if he were going to pay for his order, but he dropped it when he grabbed the cash. His stupid crime spree continued until he tried to rob *another* restaurant—with two police officers inside. It was simple to connect him to the first scene, where he had left his driver's license and birth certificate. "He made it easy to track him," says Detective Jeff McKinney.

TWO THIEVES IN LOUISIANA LED POLICE ON A **15-MILE CAR CHASE** IN A STOLEN **KRISPY KREME** TRUCK.

The largest prison in the United States is the Twin Towers Correctional Facility in Los

Angeles, California, at a sprawling 1.5 million square feet—as big as 31 football fields!

A Minnesota man broke into the restaurant where he worked after the store had closed.

Surprise CALLER

ROGERSVILLE, TENNESSEE

Emergency dispatchers couldn't believe their ears: A bad guy was on the phone talking about plans for a crime! Apparently the would-be thief accidentally pressed 9 on the cell phone tucked into his jeans, and the call went through to 911 dispatchers. Workers listened as the guy talked to his friend about their plan to rob a local business. So when the thieves tried to haul off a refrigerator stolen from the store, police were waiting outside to bust them.

IT'S ILLEGAL TO **RIDE A HORSE** FASTER THAN TEN MILES AN HOUR IN **INDIANAPOLIS, INDIANA.**

He had time to fry some chicken wings as a snack before police found him.

Um, HELLO!
SILVER SPRING, MARYLAND

AN **ALLIGATOR** BROKE INTO A FLORIDA HOME THROUGH THE **DOGGY DOOR.**

Calling all stupid crooks! After the power went out at one thief's house, he broke into someone else's home to charge his cell phone—and to swipe some valuables. When the homeowner returned unexpectedly, the burglar jumped out a window but forgot his cell phone. Investigators dialed one of the phone's frequently called numbers and, through some sneaky sleuthing, discovered the crook's name and address. They also found out that the guy had committed more than 50 burglaries. Looks like this thief's cell phone led to another cell—in jail.

When a computer glitch opened a New Zealand supermarket without any employees inside,

half of the shoppers paid at self-checkout; the other half snatched the groceries for free.

A California house cat named Dusty (aka Klepto the Cat) is a neighborhood cat burglar.

Veggie VICTIM

ASHBURTON, NEW ZEALAND

One boy will probably never want to eat peas again—he was buried up to his chest in them! When three friends got bored one day, they decided to break into a shipping container. But after they busted it open, an avalanche of dried peas poured out, trapping one boy in the veggies! Rescue workers used a forklift to free the boy—and then handed him over to police.

A PIZZA SHOP OWNER WAS ARRESTED AFTER HE **HID MICE** IN THE RESTROOMS OF COMPETING PIZZERIAS.

Dusty has stolen towels, toys, bathing suits, and about 600 shoes from neighbors' yards.

Next in LINE

BOSTON, MASSACHUSETTS

A bank robber was so focused on stealing money that he didn't even notice the police officer in the room. The would-be bank robber drew odd looks as he waited in line wearing white gloves and a scarf over his face, so a uniformed officer quietly walked up behind him. The robber was so busy passing the teller a note demanding big bills and "no funny money" that he didn't notice the officer. When the teller handed over the cash, the officer arrested the crook. Sometimes standing in line is worth the wait.

A BRITISH MAN WAS FINED £30 (ABOUT $48) FOR COMBING HIS HAIR WHILE DRIVING.

A hungry thief in the Netherlands stopped in the midst of a house robbery to fry a fish.

His meal ended when the fishy smell woke up the homeowner, who was sleeping upstairs.

Police in Ontario, Canada, arrested a brainless bad guy after he called the convenience store

DROP It!
FERNDALE, MICHIGAN

Talk about getting tripped up. This criminal was caught because his baggy pants kept falling down as he tried to run away! After the thief stole some DVDs, officers quickly gave chase. But as soon as the bad guy started running, his baggy pants fell down and he tripped! Desperate to escape, the thief finally kicked off his pants and started running in his underwear. That's when the police nabbed him. Next time maybe he'll wear a belt!

AN **OHIO MAN** WAS CITED FOR **HISSING AND BARKING** AT A **POLICE DOG.**

he planned to rob and asked how much money was in the cash register.

Grin and BEAR IT

SACRAMENTO, CALIFORNIA

IT'S AGAINST THE LAW TO DYE A DUCKLING BLUE AND OFFER IT FOR SALE IN KENTUCKY.

Police officers focus on taking a bite out of crime. But in this case, crime took a bite out of a criminal. He was caught because he left his false teeth at the scene! The crook had crashed a stolen truck into two other cars and then run away to hide. But he'd lost his false teeth, which had fallen onto the truck's floor after the crash. Police quickly found a guy who was missing his upper set of dentures and identified him as the crook. No tooth fairy is coming to visit *this* thief.

Police in Belgium caught a burglar by analyzing the DNA they gathered from smelly socks

he left at the crime scene. He had lifted a clean pair from the home he robbed.

DIRTY Driver
HOLDEN HILL, AUSTRALIA

IT'S ILLEGAL TO SPRAY SILLY STRING ON HALLOWEEN IN HOLLYWOOD, IN LOS ANGELES, CALIFORNIA.

Rule No. 12 of *The Smart Criminal's Handbook:* Don't fall asleep in a vehicle you just stole. After a thief nabbed a car in the middle of the night, he decided to park it at a 24-hour car wash so he could take a nap. But he forgot to turn off the headlights and windshield wipers. So when another customer noticed that, *plus* the fact that no one was scrubbing the vehicle, he got suspicious. He reported this odd behavior to an employee, who phoned the police. Before the cops could arrest the bad guy, they had to wake him up.

A 71-year-old grandmother—known as Supergran—stopped a daytime jewel heist in

England by hitting the five would-be thieves with her handbag.

Employees at a fried chicken restaurant in Scotland, United Kingdom, laughed a robber

Sound ASLEEP

BURNLEY, ENGLAND, IN THE UNITED KINGDOM

This criminal must have thought he was having a bad dream when he woke up in front of the cops. A woman had called police after waking up to strange noises one morning. When police arrived, they discovered the noises were from a burglar sacked out on the woman's couch. Apparently the bad guy had broken in the night before, stuffed his pants with jewelry, and then decided to take a nap before escaping. Guess if you snooze, you lose.

THE **BIGGEST** HIJACK RANSOM EVER PAID WAS **$3.2 MILLION** FOR A **STOLEN SHIP.**

out of the store because his crooked ski mask allowed him to see out of only one eye.

FAKE Fax

BLOOMINGTON, INDIANA

OVER $43 MILLION WAS STOLEN FROM 5,546 BANKS IN THE U.S. IN 2010.

This guy thought he was being smart with numbers, but he was really *dumb* with letters. A jailed criminal created a fake document stating he needed to pay only $500 instead of $100,000 to be released on bail. Then he asked a friend to fax the paperwork to the jail. The problem? The criminal misspelled the name of the county, so police knew it was a fake! Forget $100,000. When the guy was found out, officials increased his bail to *$250,000*.

After robbing a house in New Zealand, the thief broke in again to leave a written apology and

to return the loot, including a basketball and gloves he had charged to the owner's credit card.

A man started to open an account at a Pennsylvania bank. He showed the teller his ID

Straight to PRISON

OSSINING, NEW YORK

Ever heard of a thief breaking *into* prison? After several robberies, this bad guy's luck finally ran out when police spotted him and ran after him. Panicking, the thief jumped a fence—and landed right by the wall of a prison, where corrections officers promptly apprehended him. Maybe the guy was simply drawn to where he really belonged.

IT'S ILLEGAL TO **THROW BANANA PEELS** ON THE **SIDEWALKS OF MOBILE, ALABAMA.**

before robbing the bank. Needless to say, he didn't get far before police found him.

I See London, I SEE France...

SALT LAKE CITY, UTAH

This would-be thief gave new meaning to the word *undercover*—he wore underpants instead of a mask on his face. In his "disguise," the bad guy sneaked into a shop at a golf course. After an employee spotted him, the thief dashed out the door. Soon, though, two golfers riding in a cart heard the employee's calls for help and went into hot pursuit. The fearless golfers chased the crook until they knocked him down and held him for the police. Then the robber was "debriefed"!

A LAW ONCE MADE IT ILLEGAL TO **SING LOUDLY** OUTSIDE AFTER SUNSET IN **HAWAII.**

The United States had no universal emergency number until 911 was introduced in 1968.

BAD Check
ENGLEWOOD, COLORADO

Things not to hand over when robbing a bank: your name, address, and phone number. After passing the teller a note that read, "Give me all the money in your drawer now," the robber stuffed his pockets with cash. The problem? His note was written on a personal check. The thief had tried to black out his personal information, but detectives had no trouble reading his name and home address and tracked him down. Now the only place where the thief will be passing notes is in jail.

THE FEDERAL BUREAU OF INVESTIGATION (FBI) IS MORE THAN 100 YEARS OLD.

DOG Disguise
CRANBERRY TOWNSHIP, PENNSYLVANIA

IN JACKSON, MISSISSIPPI, IT IS ILLEGAL **TO GIVE AWAY LIVE GOLDFISH AS A PRIZE.**

One would-be thief *thought* he was being clever by wearing a mask that looked like Pluto the cartoon dog when robbing a grocery store. But the clerk took one look at the goofy disguise and burst out laughing! Totally humiliated, the bad guy left the store—without any cash. "We don't recommend laughing in these situations," says Sergeant Dave Kovach. "The man could have been dangerous." It looks like the "dog" found the clerk's funny bone!

Teens who were robbing stranded drivers in a blizzard got busted when they got stuck, too!

Couch CRIMINAL

SALINAS, CALIFORNIA

If you were being chased by police, the first thing you'd do is sit down and watch TV, right? That's exactly what one criminal decided to do! Police were in hot pursuit of a car thief when the bad guy suddenly crashed into a parked car and ran into a nearby house. When police entered the home, they found the thief watching television on the couch, where they arrested him. Must have been a really good show!

THE FIRST PERSON ARRESTED FOR SPEEDING IN THE UNITED STATES WAS DRIVING 12 MILES AN HOUR IN 1899.

A vandal in the U.K. got busted because he wrote his name on the wall at the crime scene.

FUNNY Money

LAFAYETTE, INDIANA

Note to fake moneymakers: Be sure you know which famous face appears on each bill! A waitress noticed that a hundred-dollar bill a customer had given her had Abraham Lincoln's face on it. But Lincoln appears on the five-dollar bill! (Benjamin Franklin is on the hundred-dollar bill.) The guy took off when the waitress called police, but detectives later caught him with other phony bills in his wallet. Instead of spending cash, he spent time in jail!

IT'S ILLEGAL TO **PREDICT THE FUTURE IN YAMHILL, OREGON.**

Thieves stole 1,500 pounds of cheese and 88 pounds of butter from a French dairy.

TOOL Box

YORK, PENNSYLVANIA

This dumb pair discovered that two criminal minds aren't better than one. After stealing some tools from a truck, a man and woman decided to sell their booty for some quick cash. Seeing a service station, the thieves headed over and asked an employee if he was interested in buying the stolen goods. But they didn't expect the guy to recognize the tools: They were his! He called police, who made sure the only tools the thieves would be using were the ones at a prison workshop.

POLICE CAN TELL IDENTICAL TWINS APART BY THEIR FINGERPRINTS.

Two students were arrested after trying to use raw chicken to lure alligators out of a pond.

Robbery REDIAL
VILLA RICA, GEORGIA

One thief thought it'd be a good idea to check in with her mom by using the phone at the house she and a friend were robbing. She was wrong! When the victim returned to her burglarized house, she was smart enough to hit redial on her phone—and the thief's mother answered. With Mom's help, police traced the thieving friends to a local motel and arrested them. "The thief did part of our job for us when she called her mom," Lieutenant Shane Taylor says. "The victim did the rest when she hit redial."

LINCOLN, NEBRASKA'S, "VACUUM BANDIT" USED A VACUUM CLEANER TO SUCK COINS OUT OF LAUNDRY MACHINES.

A kindhearted Croatian man made sandwiches for the burglar he caught robbing his home.

A robbery victim in Poland didn't have to guess who stole her furniture. She saw a

Secret SETUP
CATAWBA COUNTY, NORTH CAROLINA

This criminal sent the right text message—to the wrong person. Officers had arrested one suspect in a series of break-ins and had taken his cell phone as evidence. So when the nabbed burglar received a text message from his partner in crime, the officers read it. "R U cot yet?" the message read. "Not yet, can u come get me?" officers texted back. When the bad guy went to pick up his friend, police were waiting. "This was hilarious," Major Coy Reid says. "I still can't believe this guy texted us back."

> THE **RENO BROTHERS GANG** COMMITTED THE **FIRST ROBBERY** OF A **MOVING TRAIN** IN 1866.

photo of her neighbor sitting in her favorite armchair on a school reunion website.

Caught on CAMERA

MANCHESTER, ENGLAND, IN THE UNITED KINGDOM

A CHICAGO BUSINESSMAN **PAID $3,000** FOR A **PLASTER MOLD** OF GANGSTER JOHN DILLINGER'S **FACE.**

Police had no problem identifying a thief who tried to rip off a video camera store. Eight cameras were broadcasting his every move on display TVs in the store. Police watched footage of the thief casing the place, snatching a laptop computer, and then fleeing. Thanks to the cameras, police quickly caught the thief. "When I watched the tape of him jumping up several times to look through the front window, I had to laugh," says store owner David Arathoon.

A New Zealand man returned home to find a real-life Goldilocks asleep in his bed. She had

broken into his house, eaten his food, and even tried on his clothes, before taking a nap.

A tidy thief in the United Kingdom stole $200,000 worth of goods from 105 homes over

Knock, KNOCK!

WOODBINE, GEORGIA

What did one crook do after escaping from jail? He came back! Three inmates had forced open the back door of the jail to release a fourth prisoner. After escaping prison grounds, the prisoner broke into a convenience store and stole some goodies to bring back to his three "friends." But when he returned, they'd locked him out. Instead of escaping for good, the inmate looked for a way back into jail, and a guard spotted him. "He was afraid he'd be in trouble," Captain Larry Hamilton says. "He was right!"

IT'S ILLEGAL TO **OWN A SMELLY DOG** IN GALESBURG, ILLINOIS.

ten months. But he often washed the dishes before leaving the scene of the crime.

RUNNING ON Empty

COOKEVILLE, TENNESSEE

A getaway car is no good if you can't get away. When officers responded to reports of a suspicious truck at a store, they found the vehicle in the parking lot with a stolen recliner in the back—and three suspects inside. Apparently the crooks hadn't noticed the truck was low on gas when they'd pulled into the parking lot. They ran out of gas when they tried to leave! The crooks were so shocked they just sat there. "These guys weren't great planners," Captain David Dukes says.

THE LONGEST JAIL SENTENCE TOTALED MORE THAN 11,000 YEARS.

United States court of law. These dogs were the first animals to have this honor.

A thief tried to snatch a new wardrobe from a Dumpster filled with donated clothes,

SWEET Ride
CHARLES COUNTY, MARYLAND

Maybe next time these guys will be a little more stealthy. After robbing a store, two thieves jumped into a very noticeable getaway vehicle: an ice-cream truck! When a sheriff's deputy spotted it speeding down the highway at nearly 10 p.m.—way past an ice-cream truck's bedtime—he followed it. The crooks tried to outrace the deputy but crashed instead, and their chances of freedom melted away.

A **BURGLAR** HID FROM POLICE BY PLAYING DEAD IN A COFFIN; **HE BLEW HIS COVER BY BREATHING.**

but he got trapped inside instead. Police arrested him after a four-hour rescue effort.

NOT So Fast
DOVER, NEW HAMPSHIRE

IT WAS ONCE ILLEGAL TO **SELL DOUGHNUT HOLES** IN **LEIGH, NEBRASKA.**

You've heard of a getaway car. But a getaway lawn mower? That's exactly what one criminal tried to use to escape the scene of a crime. After vandalizing a building, the bad guy puttered away on a riding lawn mower. Police were in hot pursuit but didn't stop the guy until one cruiser finally blocked the mower's path. "Most police chases are high speed," Captain Tony Colarusso says. "This one was low speed."

The Great Train Robbery of 1963—in which thieves stole £2.6 million (more than

$4 million) from a mail train—was likely the largest heist on the British railroad.

WANTED

POLICE EXAM Here

During a nighttime restaurant robbery, a New Jersey thief decided he needed a nap and

Flunking the TEST

CHULA VISTA, CALIFORNIA

This guy couldn't decide if he wanted to be a crook or a police officer. A thief ran away after shoplifting, but police tracked him down with help from the bad guy's former roommates. A detective called the thief and tried to get him to admit to his crime. The thief mentioned he was taking an exam to become a police officer. Later, when the crook showed up for the test, an officer told him to walk to a separate room. He thought it was part of the hiring process—but really it was part of the arresting process.

POLICE ARRESTED A **MUGGER** AFTER HE CHECKED OUT HIS **REFLECTION** IN A SECURITY CAMERA'S LENS.

fell asleep on top of the refrigerator. His loud snoring led police right to him.

Snack
BANDITS
ST. PAUL, MINNESOTA

Hansel and Gretel left a trail of bread crumbs to follow. These dumb crooks left a trail of cheese curls. Police investigating a shattered vending machine at a recreation center found the snacks missing, and a trail of orange cheese curls led them all the way to a nearby house. Officers found the stolen snacks in a closet and busted the crooks. These guys should have listened when their moms told them, "No snacking between meals."

The term "bootleg," which means "to make, distribute, or sell something illegally," comes from

the 17th century, when high boots were in style—and an easy place to hide illegal goods.

Police quickly found an Illinois bank robber because she wrote a note demanding money

Not-So-Dirty CROOK

PORTLAND, OREGON

Criminals usually don't ask police for help—but this guy called the cops on himself. The man had broken into a house and decided to clean himself up in the shower before leaving. When the home-owner returned, she questioned the burglar and called police. But the bad guy was so afraid that he called police, too! Guess taking a shower is not the best way to make a clean getaway.

MURPHY THE SPRINGER SPANIEL WAS THE FIRST DOG TO SNIFF OUT ILLEGAL CELL PHONES IN PRISONS.

on the back of a paper with her name on it, and then left her debit card on the counter.

POLICE Lineup

NEW WESTMINSTER, CANADA

ORANGUTANS, THE ESCAPE ARTISTS OF ZOOS, ARE KNOWN FOR FINDING WAYS TO BREAK OUT OF THEIR ENCLOSURES.

It's not very smart to commit a crime across the street from a police station. But it's even dumber to do it while officers are standing behind you. After saying hello to a man outside a coffee shop across the road from their station, two cops went inside to order their drinks. When the man entered the shop a few minutes later, he cut in line and demanded money from the cashier—right in front of the officers. Before the officers could pick up their coffee, they picked up the would-be robber and hauled him away.

The Birdman of Alcatraz—a notorious prisoner whose real name was Robert Stroud—

got his nickname because he had kept birds in his cell at another prison.

After a chatty train traveler refused to stop talking on her cell phone in the quiet car

Open and SHUT

FRESNO, CALIFORNIA

One criminal was happy to see sheriff's deputies when they rescued him from a locked car trunk. The criminal told deputies he had been kidnapped and stashed in the trunk. But they soon figured out that the guy—surrounded by stereo equipment and other items he had stolen from another car—had crawled into the trunk to steal more stuff. When he had grabbed the trunk lid to pull himself out, the lid had closed, locking him in! "When they were handing out brains, he must have forgotten to show up," says Lieutenant Toby Rien.

IN MASSACHUSETTS IT IS ILLEGAL TO DRIVE A HORSE-DRAWN SLEIGH WITH FEWER THAN THREE BELLS ON THE HARNESS.

during a 16-hour trip, police arrested the woman and escorted her off the train.

Ya Snooze, Ya Lose

MONROE, WASHINGTON

It's never a good idea to fall asleep on the job. After a break-in at a department store, police officers started following a trail of stolen items. About 200 feet from the store's parking lot, they stumbled upon backpacks, hammocks, chair cushions—*and* the two thieves who had stolen the property and had fallen fast asleep in a field. One was resting his head on a chair cushion; the other was snuggled up on a hammock he'd laid on the ground. When police woke them, the crooks must have thought it was a bad dream.

BOTNETS— REMOTE-CONTROLLED COMPUTER VIRUSES— INFECTED TWO MILLION COMPUTERS IN APRIL 2011.

A man broke into a Colorado house, stole a bear-shaped bar of soap, and then hid in the attic.

A young man was charged with theft after he stole a lawn mower from a school and rode it

Baring It ALL

LAPEL, INDIANA

This shoplifter thought her pants would be the perfect hiding place for her loot, but the pants had a different idea. After the thief stuffed several sweet treats down her leggings, the store owner got wise and grabbed her by her hood. As she struggled to get away, her treat-filled pants fell to the ground! The police arriving on the scene brought handcuffs—and hopefully some tighter pants and suspenders!

CIVILIAN TIPS HAVE LED TO THE ARREST OF MORE THAN 150 FUGITIVES ON THE FBI'S MOST WANTED LIST.

three miles to his parents' house, where he cut the grass in the middle of the night.

Hot PROPERTY
ANTWERP, BELGIUM

When store detectives noticed that a woman had suddenly grown much bigger than she had been when she arrived, they knew something was up. Turns out the woman was trying to steal clothes by wearing them out of the store! Even though it was a hot summer day, the thief piled on a jogging suit, a sweater, 11 tops, shorts, and a pair of sneakers all at once! But the detectives were too smart for this bulked-up shoplifter. She was sent back to the dressing room, and then straight to the police station.

IT'S ILLEGAL TO HAVE A **PIZZA DELIVERED** TO SOMEONE WHO DIDN'T ORDER IT IN **LOUISIANA.**

HANDS Off

KEY LARGO, FLORIDA

A PARROT SCARED OFF HOUSE BURGLARS BY LETTING OUT A MIGHTY SQUAWK AT 4 a.m.

If there's one thing you *don't* want people knowing about you, it's that you've recently had your hand on a toilet seat. But that's exactly how this criminal got caught. Called to the scene of a home robbery, detectives discovered a palm print the burglar had left on the potty and identified the crook through a prints database. Police don't think the thief needed a bathroom break, though. The toilet was below the window that the bad guy had broken in to. Let's hope he at least washed his hands.

A German cyclist was arrested after asking police for directions while riding a stolen bike.

High-Speed CHASE

MONROE, OHIO

I f you lose your getaway car, don't ask the police to help you get it back. Police were in hot pursuit of a thief after he loaded his truck with stolen frozen pizzas from a warehouse. After a chase, the crook crashed his truck into a fence and ran off. The next day, he reported the truck stolen—even though police had seen him driving the truck! Instead of getting his truck back, the thief got arrested. Looks like his face wasn't as forgettable as he thought.

A CALIFORNIA MAN ILLEGALLY **CAUGHT 6 LOBSTERS.** HE STUFFED THEM **DOWN HIS PANTS** WHEN THE POLICE SHOWED UP.

Notorious mobster Al Capone's business card said he was a used furniture salesman.

Money TRAIL

FRESNO, WISCONSIN

It wasn't hard to track down *these* two thieves—especially with the trail of coins they left behind! Two men stole $785 in bills and coins from a convenience store and stashed the cash in a milk crate. But as they were running from the store, the coins fell through the holes in the crate! Police looking for telltale footprints in the snow also found a path of nickels, dimes, and quarters. They followed the coin trail right to the robbers' front door. Busted!

IN FLORIDA IT'S ILLEGAL TO LEAVE A REFRIGERATOR ON THE SIDE OF THE ROAD.

Police in Australia caught a thief by tracing the DNA he had left on a half-eaten doughnut.

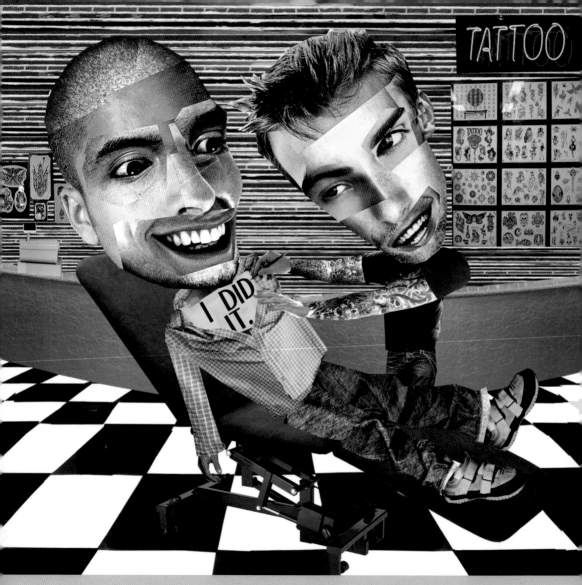

INK That Stinks

PICO RIVERA, CALIFORNIA

Here's a way to tip off police that you committed a crime: have the scene tattooed on your chest. After a gang member was arrested for another illegal act, an investigator thought he recognized the criminal's tattoo. Turns out the art showed the scene of an unsolved crime the bad guy had been involved in. So an undercover detective pretended to be a gangster and got the dumb dude to brag about what he *thought* he had gotten away with. Busted!

IN PIRATE LINGO "BUCKO" MEANS "FRIEND."

In Mobile, Alabama, it is illegal to wear a mask in public, except to celebrate Mardi Gras.

Bank Fraud
FAIRFIELD, CONNECTICUT

A THIEF IN POLAND WAS FOUND ASLEEP ON A TOILET IN THE STORE HE HAD ROBBED.

Two crooks were in such a hurry for some fast cash, they phoned ahead to tell a bank that they'd swing by to steal $100,000. Smart bank officials contacted police before the crooks arrived, so when one robber exited the bank with the cash, officers were there to greet him—with handcuffs. Other officers nabbed his partner in the getaway car. Says Sergeant James Perez of the Fairfield Police Department, "They definitely weren't the sharpest tools in the shed."

The term "white-collar crime," coined in 1939, refers to fraud committed by business

and government officials, who traditionally wear white shirts with collars.

The infamous pirate Blackbeard seized 1,500 pounds of gold and silver during his 1718

All LOCKED Up

LAKE CITY, FLORIDA

After a thief broke into a car, the owners—alerted to the break-in by a neighbor—grabbed their car keys and hurried outside. When the crook saw the couple approaching, he tried to exit the car. But the owner was too fast. He pressed the automatic lock button on the car's remote key system to trap the crook inside. Again and again the bad guy unlocked the door, but the owner locked it again before he could escape. The crook finally put up his hands in surrender and waited for the police to arrive.

POLICE PULLED OVER A BRITISH MAN FOR **LAUGHING WHILE DRIVING, BUT LATER LET HIM GO.**

blockade of Charleston, South Carolina. That's worth about $359,000 in today's money!

You Hide, We Seek

NORTH EAST, MARYLAND

When a convenience store manager arrived at work, he heard a strange sound in the ventilation system and spotted something even stranger: a pair of legs dangling from an air duct! Turns out the would-be thief got stuck on his way in, but that's not what he told firefighters. "He said he was playing hide-and-seek with friends, which we absolutely didn't believe," says Sergeant Michael Holmes of the Cecil County Sheriff's Department. Guess this crook wasn't trapped long enough to think up a good excuse!

IN NEW HAMPSHIRE IT'S ILLEGAL TO **COLLECT SEAWEED** AT NIGHT.

A Mississippi pharmacist fooled a thief who kept stealing prescription pills from his store.

He filled the prescription bottle with kidney beans instead of the pills the criminal was after.

An Ohio couple was caught river rafting without life jackets during a flood warning. The

CASH Refund

BROOKLYN, NEW YORK

After swiping money from an apartment, one burglar realized that he had left his wallet behind. He tried to come back in through the window, but the resident had returned home and asked what the thief was doing. "He said he needed to use the bathroom," Yaakov Kanelsky says. Kanelsky wouldn't let him back inside. So the criminal ran to the front door and started shoving the money under it, offering the cash in exchange for his wallet. Kanelsky had already called police. Guess he didn't think that was a fair exchange.

A MAN IN FRANCE **STOLE 240,000 OYSTERS—** LIKELY THE NATION'S BIGGEST **SHELLFISH THEFT EVER.**

93299

COUNTY
JAIL

Want more weird?
See page 174!

Illustrations are indicated by **boldface.**

ABOUT THE ARTIST

"Working on Stupid Criminals is so much fun! While the faces in these collages are not based on any actual people, details such as the model of car or the people's clothing are sometimes based on real events. To make these crazy collages, I start with a line drawing and layer pieces of collage on top. Backgrounds can start as torn paper doodles and then become landscapes or interiors. It's amazing what you can make from a scrap of paper!"

—*Tom Nick Cocotos*

Check out the artist online!
cocotos.com

Based on the "Stupid Criminals" department in
National Geographic Kids magazine:
Rachel Buchholz, *Executive Editor*
Nicole Lazarus, *Art Director*
Margaret Krauss, *Assistant Editor*

Published by the National Geographic Society
John M. Fahey, Jr., *Chairman of the Board and
    Chief Executive Officer*
Timothy T. Kelly, *President*
Declan Moore, *Executive Vice President;
    President, Publishing*
Melina Gerosa Bellows, *Executive Vice President;
    Chief Creative Officer, Books, Kids, and Family*

Prepared by the Book Division
Hector Sierra, *Senior Vice President,
    and General Manager*
Nancy Laties Feresten, *Senior Vice President,
    Editor in Chief, Children's Books*
Jonathan Halling, *Design Director, Books and
    Children's Publishing*
Jay Sumner, *Director of Photography, Children's Publishing*
Jennifer Emmett, *Editorial Director, Children's Books*
Eva Absher-Schantz, *Managing Art Director,
    Children's Publishing*
Carl Mehler, *Director of Maps*
R. Gary Colbert, *Production Director*
Jennifer A. Thornton, *Managing Editor*

Staff for This Book
Robin Terry, *Project Editor*
Eva Absher-Schantz, *Art Director*
Jay Sumner, *Photo Director*
Ruthie Thompson, *Designer*
Jeannette Kimmel, Meg Weaver, *Researchers*
Kate Olesin, *Assistant Editor*
Kathryn Robbins, *Design Production Assistant*
Hillary Moloney, *Illustrations Assistant*
Elisabeth Deffner, Kimberly Forkner, Erin Taylor Monroney,
    Amanda Pressner, *Contributing Writers*
Grace Hill, *Associate Managing Editor*
Joan Gossett, *Production Editor*
Lewis R. Bassford, *Production Manager*
Susan Borke, *Legal and Business Affairs*

Manufacturing and Quality Management
Christopher A. Liedel, *Chief Financial Officer*
Phillip L. Schlosser, *Senior Vice President*
Chris Brown, *Technical Director*
Nicole Elliott, *Manager*
Rachel Faulise, *Manager*
Robert L. Barr, *Manager*

The National Geographic Society is one of the world's largest nonprofit scientific and educational organizations. Founded in 1888 to increase and diffuse geographic knowledge, the Society works to inspire people to care about the planet. National Geographic reflects the world through its magazines, television programs, films, music and radio, books, DVDs, maps, exhibitions, live events, school publishing programs, interactive media and merchandise. *National Geographic* magazine, the Society's official journal, published in English and 33 local-language editions, is read by more than 38 million people each month. The National Geographic Channel reaches 320 million households in 34 languages in 166 countries. National Geographic Digital Media receives more than 15 million visitors a month. National Geographic has funded more than 9,400 scientific research, conservation and exploration projects and supports an education program promoting geography literacy. For more information, visit nationalgeographic.com.

For more information, please call 1-800-NGS LINE (647-5463) or write to the following address:

National Geographic Society
1145 17th Street N.W.
Washington, D.C. 20036-4688 U.S.A.

Visit us online at nationalgeographic.com/books

For librarians and teachers: ngchildrensbooks.org

More for kids from National Geographic:
kids.nationalgeographic.com

For information about special discounts for bulk purchases, please contact National Geographic Books Special Sales: ngspecsales@ngs.org

For rights or permissions inquiries, please contact National Geographic Books Subsidiary Rights:
ngbookrights@ngs.org

ISBN: 978-1-4263-0861-1

Printed in China

12/RRDS/1

Collect all of the books in the Weird But True series!

AVAILABLE IN DECEMBER 2012!

DOWNLOAD
the NEW *National Geographic Kids Weird But True* for iPhone®, iPod touch®, and iPad®!

Available on the App Store